The Life and Ideas of a Wise Emperor

A Fun Book for Curious K

Meet Thomas Aquinas!

📌 01 - Introduction

01

Welcome to the world of Thomas Aquinas, one of the greatest thinkers in history!
In this section, we will discover who he was, why he loved asking big questions, and how his ideas still inspire young minds today.

📌 02 - The Life of Thomas Aquinas

02

🔹 A Curious Child - Learn about Thomas' early years, his love for learning, and how he was different from his family of knights.
🔹 The Tower of Learning - Discover why his family locked him away in a castle and how he never stopped thinking and learning.
🔹 The Great Escape - How Thomas found his way to a monastery, following his true calling to study and seek wisdom.
🔹 From Student to Teacher - Follow Thomas' journey as he learned from great scholars and became a teacher himself.

📌 03 - The Greatest Ideas of Thomas Aquinas

03

💡 Faith & Reason Together - Thomas believed that faith and knowledge could work as a team, not as enemies.
📖 Summa Theologica - Discover the famous book Thomas wrote, answering some of life's biggest questions.
🛡 Wisdom is Greater than Strength - Why Thomas believed that knowledge and kindness were more powerful than swords.
✨ The Power of Asking Questions - How his way of thinking changed philosophy, education, and even science!

Who Was Thomas Aquinas?

A long time ago, in a big castle in Italy, a little boy was born. His name? Thomas Aquinas!

From the moment he could talk, Thomas loved asking questions.

"Why is the sky blue?"

"How do we know what is right or wrong?"

"Can thinking help us understand the world?"

While other kids played with toy swords, Thomas sat under trees reading scrolls and thinking deeply.

His parents wanted him to grow up to be a great knight, but Thomas had a different dream—he wanted to learn everything!

Even though people didn't understand his love for books, Thomas believed that big questions lead to big discoveries!

Great thinkers start by asking big questions!

What is something you've always been curious about?

Thomas
he Aquimas
ane to
the nef llove..!

A Mind Full of Big Ideas!

Thomas wasn't like the other boys in his family.
His father and brothers were knights, strong and brave, trained to fight in battles.
"Wouldn't you like to be a knight too?" his father asked.
Thomas thought for a moment, then shook his head.
"I want to be a scholar, not a soldier!" he said.
His brothers laughed.
"Books won't protect a kingdom!" they said.
"A wise ruler needs more than swords," Thomas replied. "He needs knowledge!"
But Thomas' big ideas were just getting started. He would grow up to change the way people think about wisdom, faith, and learning.
He believed that faith and reason could work together, not against each other.
His ideas were so powerful that they are still studied today—over 700 years later!

You don't have to follow the crowd–follow what you love!

Have you ever liked something different from what others expect?

The Ideas That Changed the World

Thomas Aquinas didn't just ask big questions—he found big answers! Even today, his ideas continue to inspire students, teachers, and leaders all over the world.

📖 What did he teach us?

💡 Faith and Reason Work Together

Some people thought that faith and science should be separate, but Thomas believed they could help each other.

"Faith tells us why. Reason tells us how." - Thomas Aquinas

📖 Education is for Everyone

Before Thomas, only a few people were allowed to study deep ideas. But he believed anyone could learn, no matter who they were!

🛡 Wisdom is More Powerful Than Strength

Many rulers used weapons to lead, but Thomas taught that a wise leader uses knowledge, kindness, and truth.

✨ Great Ideas Never Disappear

His famous book, Summa Theologica, has been studied for over 700 years! Scientists, philosophers, and even astronauts have learned from his wisdom!

Even though Thomas lived long ago, his ideas still help us understand the world today.

And guess what? YOU can ask big questions just like him!

A Very Curious Boy

A long time ago, in a big castle in Italy, a baby boy was born.
His name? Thomas Aquinas!
His family was rich and powerful, and they wanted Thomas to grow up to be a great knight. They imagined him riding a horse, wearing shiny armor, and fighting in battles.
But Thomas? Oh no—he had a different kind of adventure in mind!
Instead of playing with swords, he liked books. Instead of practicing how to fight, he spent hours asking questions.
"Why is the sky blue?"
"Where does the wind come from?"
"How do we know what is right or wrong?"
His parents chuckled and said, "Thomas, you think too much!"
But Thomas loved thinking! He believed that every great answer starts with a question.

Great thinkers start by asking big questions!

What is something you've always been curious about?

A Family of Warriors, A Boy Who Loved Books

In Thomas' family, everyone was strong and brave. His father and brothers were all knights, trained to fight and protect the land.

One day, his father asked, "Thomas, wouldn't you like to be a knight like your brothers?"

Thomas thought for a moment, then shook his head.

"I want to be a scholar, not a soldier!" he said.

His brothers laughed.

"Books won't protect a kingdom!" they said.

"A wise ruler needs more than swords," Thomas replied. "He needs knowledge!"

His family didn't understand why Thomas loved books more than battles. But Thomas wasn't afraid to be different. Deep inside, he knew that wisdom was the greatest power of all!

You don't have to follow the crowd–follow what you love!

Have you ever liked something different from what others expect?

A Big Decision

As Thomas grew older, he made a surprising choice. Instead of training to be a knight, he wanted to become a monk—a person who studies, prays, and teaches others. His mother was worried. "Thomas, are you sure? Monks live simply. No castles, no feasts, no riches!"

But Thomas smiled.

"I don't need riches, Mother. I need knowledge!"

His father was not happy. He had dreamed of his son becoming a great warrior, not a man in a robe reading books all day!

So, the family came up with a plan.

"If we can't change Thomas' mind, we'll keep him here until he forgets about becoming a monk!"

And just like that, they locked him away in the family tower!

Courage is standing up for what you believe in!

Have you ever made a choice that others didn't understand?

A Boy in a Tower

For one whole year, Thomas was stuck in the tall stone tower.

No books.

No teachers.

No way to leave.

His family hoped he would change his mind. But Thomas? Oh no!

Instead of giving up, he turned his prison into a classroom.

- He thought deeply about all the questions in his mind.
- He prayed for guidance.
- He even made up lessons to teach himself!

One day, his mother felt sorry for him. She secretly helped him escape through a small window.

Thomas ran away—not to battle, not to a kingdom, but to a place where he could learn all he wanted.

He had finally found his true path!

Even when things seem difficult, never stop learning!

If you were locked in a tower, what would you do to stay hopeful?

A New Home for Learning

After escaping, Thomas joined a group of monks called the Dominicans. They were kind and wise, and they welcomed Thomas with open arms.

For the first time, he felt truly at home.

- He woke up early to study books.
- He asked even bigger questions.
- He wrote down everything he learned, so he would never forget.

But not everyone was kind to Thomas.

At the university, some students thought he was too quiet. They called him "The Dumb Ox" because he didn't talk much.

But what they didn't know was this: Thomas wasn't dumb at all—he was just thinking!

One day, his teacher, Albert the Great, heard the students teasing Thomas.

He smiled and said, "You may call him an ox now, but soon, his ideas will roar across the world!"

And you know what? He was right.

True happiness comes from following your passion!

What place makes you feel safe and happy to learn?

TOUMASLIBRRARY

The Quiet Student with Big Ideas

Now that Thomas was free to study, he worked harder than ever.

At the University of Paris, he spent hours in the library, surrounded by books taller than he was!

He read about philosophy, science, faith, and logic. He didn't just memorize facts—he wanted to understand everything.

But because he was so quiet, other students still called him "The Dumb Ox."

"Thomas never speaks!" they whispered.

"Maybe he doesn't know anything!"

But they were very wrong.

Thomas wasn't silent because he didn't know things—he was silent because he was thinking deeply!

Great thinkers don't always speak the loudest!

Have you ever been quiet but full of big ideas?

The Moment That Changed Everything

One day, during a philosophy class, the teacher asked a difficult question.

The room was silent. No one knew the answer.

Then, Thomas slowly stood up.

At first, the students laughed.

"What is he going to say?"

But then, Thomas spoke.

His words were clear, wise, and full of deep understanding.

He explained things in a way that made complicated ideas sound simple.

The students stopped laughing.

They listened.

They learned.

From that day on, no one called him 'The Dumb Ox' anymore.

They knew he was one of the smartest people in the whole university!

When you speak with wisdom, people listen!

Have you ever surprised people by showing what you know?

The Philosopher and the Big Questions

As Thomas studied more, he asked even bigger questions:

💡 What is truth?

💡 How can we tell right from wrong?

💡 Can science and faith work together?

Most people thought that faith and reason were opposites.
But Thomas believed they were friends!
"Faith tells us why. Reason tells us how." he said.
"Together, they help us find the truth!"
This idea was new and surprising!
Some people thought Thomas was too bold.
"You can't mix philosophy and religion!" they told him.
But Thomas was not afraid to think differently.
He knew that great ideas always start as questions!

Big questions lead to great discoveries!

If you could ask one BIG question, what would it be?

Writing the Greatest Book

Thomas didn't just think—he wrote!
He wrote so much that his books filled entire shelves!
But his most famous book was called Summa Theologica (soo-mah thee-oh-lo-gee-kah).
It was HUGE! More than 3,500 pages long!
Inside, Thomas explained his biggest ideas:

📖 How to live a good life
📖 How to tell right from wrong
📖 How faith and reason work together

His book was so clear and powerful that even today, people still study it all over the world!
But while Thomas was writing, something unexpected happened...

Great ideas take time and effort!

If you could write a book, what would it be about?

The King's Invitation

One day, a messenger from the King arrived.
"Thomas Aquinas, the King of France requests your wisdom!"
The King had heard about Thomas' brilliant mind and wanted his advice on important matters.
But when Thomas arrived at the palace, the King noticed something surprising.
Unlike the rich nobles, Thomas wore simple clothes.
Unlike the greedy men at court, Thomas was not impressed by gold or power.
At dinner, when servants brought out a huge feast, Thomas didn't even notice—he was too busy thinking!
The King laughed and said,
"Thomas, what are you thinking about?"
Thomas looked up, smiled, and replied,
"Something much more important than food, Your Majesty!"
Everyone laughed, but they also respected him.
They saw that Thomas cared about truth more than riches.

The best leaders are also great teachers.

Would you rather have gold or knowledge?
Why?

A Teacher for the World

After meeting the King, Thomas was asked to teach at universities across Europe.

Everywhere he went, students crowded around him to hear his lessons.

He never shouted or acted strict.

Instead, he asked his students questions:

"What do YOU think?"

"How would YOU explain this?"

He believed that the best teachers don't just give answers—they help others find them.

Even kings, bishops, and scientists came to hear his wisdom!

One student once said,

"Thomas, you make learning easy!"

Thomas smiled and replied,

"Because knowledge is meant to be shared!"

The best teachers help others find the answers!

Have you ever taught something to a friend?

The Greatest Debate

One day, Thomas was invited to a great debate. Scholars, priests, and philosophers from all over came to discuss big ideas.

Many people argued loudly about science, faith, and reason. Some believed that philosophy and religion should never mix.

Then, Thomas stood up.

At first, the room went quiet.

Then he spoke—not with anger, but with calm wisdom.

"Faith and reason are not enemies," he said.

"They are like two wings that help us fly toward the truth!"

His words were so clear and powerful that even those who disagreed with him listened closely.

When he finished, there was a moment of silence.

Then, the great scholars nodded. They knew that Thomas was not just a thinker—he was a teacher of truth.

Wisdom is found in listening and understanding!

Have you ever had to explain something to someone who disagreed with you?

The Man Who Walked Away from Fame

As Thomas' fame grew, people wanted to honor him. The Pope invited him to Rome. Kings wanted to reward him with gold.

But Thomas didn't care about power or riches.

One day, while praying, he had a mystical experience—something so amazing that he couldn't even describe it.

After that, he stopped writing.

"Everything I have written is just straw compared to what I have seen," he said.

No one knew exactly what he meant. But one thing was clear:

Thomas had spent his whole life seeking the truth—and now, he felt he had found it.

True wisdom values truth over wealth!

If you were offered riches or knowledge, which would you choose?

The Final Journey

Not long after, Thomas was invited to a great meeting of church leaders.

But on the way there, he became very sick.

The monks took him to a small monastery, where they cared for him.

Even in his final days, Thomas remained peaceful and wise.

One young monk asked, "Master Thomas, what is the most important thing you have learned?"

Thomas smiled weakly and said,

"That wisdom is nothing without kindness."

And with that, the great philosopher passed away at the age of 49.

But his ideas? Oh, they would live forever.

The greatest minds never stop seeking the truth!

What is something you want to learn more about?

Thomas

The Book That Changed the World

After Thomas died, his students collected his writings, lessons, and ideas.
His book, Summa Theologica, became one of the most important books in history.
It was studied in universities, churches, and schools for centuries.
Even today, scientists, teachers, and leaders still read his work to understand philosophy, faith, and logic.
His ideas helped shape modern education, law, and ethics!
His greatest lesson?

💡 "Always ask questions."

💡 "Seek the truth with both your heart and mind."

Great ideas live on forever!

If you could write a book that people would read for centuries, what would it be about?

Summa
Theologica

What Would Thomas Say to You?

Even though Thomas lived 700 years ago, his wisdom is still important today!

If he were here, he might ask you:

📖 What is something you are curious about?

📖 How do you know what is right or wrong?

📖 What big questions do YOU want to explore?

Because guess what? You can be a philosopher too!

All you have to do is keep asking questions, keep learning, and keep seeking truth.

Curiosity is the first step to wisdom!

What big question do you have about the world?

You Are a Philosopher Too!

Thomas started out as a curious child, just like you.
He didn't want riches or fame—he wanted knowledge and wisdom.

And now? It's YOUR turn to think deeply, ask big questions, and discover the world!

💡 Your challenge:

- Ask a big question today.
- Try to find an answer!
- Share your ideas with a friend or family member.

Who knows? Maybe one day, YOUR ideas will change the world too!

🎉 The End... Or Just the Beginning? 🎉

Every great thinker starts as a curious child—just like you!

What's one question you want to explore today?

Made in the USA
Monee, IL
04 March 2025

13428328R00026